21st
Century
Skills Library

COOL MILITARY CAREERS

AIRCRAFT PILOT

JOSH GREGORY

Published in the United States of America by
Cherry Lake Publishing, Ann Arbor, Michigan
www.cherrylakepublishing.com

Content Adviser
Cynthia Watson, PhD, author of *U.S. National Security*

Credits
Cover and page 1, ©aarrows/Shutterstock, Inc.; page 4, U.S. Air Force photo by Staff
Sgt. Larry E. Reid Jr./Released; pages 6 and 9, ©Classic Image/Alamy; page 10, U.S.
Air Force photo by Staff Sgt. Eric Harris/Released; pages 12 and 17, U.S. Air Force
photo by Tech. Sgt. Jacob N. Bailey/Released; page 15, U.S. Air Force photo by Staff
Sgt. Christopher Boitz/Released; page 18, ©Blend Images/Alamy; page 20, U.S. Air
Force photo by Staff Sgt. Chad Trujillo/Released; page 23, DoD photo by Cherie Cullen/
Released; page 24, U.S. Air Force photo by James M. Bowman/Released; page 26, U.S.
Air Force photo by Master Sgt. William Greer/Released; page 29, U.S. Air Force photo
by Airman 1st Class Camilla Griffin/Released

Library of Congress Cataloging-in-Publication Data
Gregory, Josh.
  Aircraft pilot/by Josh Gregory.
     p. cm.—(Cool military careers) (21st century skills library)
  Includes bibliographical references and index.
  Audience: Grades 4–6.
  ISBN 978-1-61080-444-8 (lib. bdg.) — ISBN 978-1-61080-531-5 (e-book) —
ISBN 978-1-61080-618-3 (pbk.)
  1. Air pilots, Military—United States—Juvenile literature. 2. United States—Armed
Forces—Vocational guidance—Juvenile literature. I. Title.
  UG793.G74 2012
  358.4'133—dc23   2012001719

Cherry Lake Publishing would like to acknowledge
the work of The Partnership for 21st Century Skills.
Please visit *www.21stcenturyskills.org* for more information.

Printed in the United States of America
Corporate Graphics Inc.
July 2012
CLFA11

TABLE OF CONTENTS

AIRCRAFT PILOT

CHAPTER ONE
SKY HIGH

"Wow!" Pete said as he pointed toward the sky. "Look at that one!" High above the ground, a group of fighter jets twisted and turned as they shot through the air at

At air shows, military pilots perform incredible tricks and fly in exciting formations.

incredible speeds. Pete's parents had taken him to an air show. All afternoon, he watched as different **aircraft** performed tricks for the crowd. Pete had never seen anything like it before. He was amazed at how fast the pilots flew their jets and how they performed such hair-raising **maneuvers**.

"Do you think I could be a pilot someday?" Pete asked his dad.

"Of course!" Pete's dad replied. "But it will take a lot of hard work and practice."

"All that hard work would be worth it if I got to fly planes like that," Pete replied.

"Yes," said Pete's dad, "but remember that being a pilot isn't all fun and games. Pilots do a lot more than just fly planes at air shows. If you want to fly planes like those, you'll have to join the military."

■ ■ ■

U.S. military pilots fly the world's most advanced aircraft. They plan and fly missions to preserve peace in foreign nations, protect the United States from its enemies, and gather information. Many of them also spend time training other pilots. Like all members of the military, pilots are dedicated to their jobs. They spend much of their time learning about new aircraft technology and preparing for future missions.

In the early 1900s, inventors Orville and Wilbur Wright had the idea to add an engine to a glider and create a powered aircraft. The Wright brothers were finally successful on December 17, 1903, when Orville flew 120 feet (37 meters) in about 12 seconds.

About four years later, the U.S. Army formed an aeronautical division to oversee the military's use of flying vehicles. At first, the Aeronautical Division was mainly

The Wright brothers' earliest aircraft could fly only short distances.

interested in using hot air balloons and **dirigibles**. But by 1909, the Army had its first airplanes. Brave pilots began experimenting with the new aircraft. As years passed, airplanes became increasingly important to the Army. President Woodrow Wilson saw the importance of air combat during World War I (1914–1918). He created the Army Air Service in 1918. By the time the war ended less than a year later, the Air Service had grown to include almost 200,000 men and 12,000 new aircraft.

LEARNING & INNOVATION SKILLS

When the U.S. Army purchased its first airplanes in 1909, there were no flight schools or trainers to teach pilots to fly. They had to learn on their own. Captain Benjamin D. Foulois was one of the first men in the Army to fly a plane. He taught himself how to operate the new technology by writing letters to the Wright brothers and asking them questions about their invention. Foulois's hard work and determination make him a strong role model for today's pilots.

In June 1941, the U.S. Department of War split the Army into the Army Air Forces and the Army Ground Forces. Six months later, the United States entered World War II (1939–1945). Once again, aircraft played a major role in the victory won by the United States and its allies. U.S. fighter planes engaged in **dogfights** with enemy aircraft. Bomber planes dropped explosives on enemy countries. In 1947, the government created the Air Force. It would be its own branch of the military, along with the Army and the Navy.

Today, the U.S. military has five branches. They are the U.S. Army, Navy, Marine Corps, Air Force, and Coast Guard. Each branch uses a variety of aircraft in different ways. The Air Force is the military's main air combat force. Its pilots fly fighters, bombers, and **stealth** planes to help the U.S. achieve victory in conflicts around the world. Interestingly, the Air Force now trains more people to operate unmanned flying **drones** in combat areas than it trains traditional pilots. The Navy uses airplanes and helicopters to assist the U.S. military at sea. They search for enemy submarines and mines and help fight enemy navies. The Marine Corps uses helicopters and airplanes for similar purposes. The Army uses few airplanes, but it does use helicopters to assist in many missions.

Bomber planes played an important role in World War II.

CHAPTER TWO
MISSION BRIEFING

A pilot's day-to-day activities can vary greatly, but there is always important work that must be done. Most active members of the military live on military bases. Some of

Some flight simulators are very similar to video games.

these bases are located in the United States, but many are in other countries around the world. A pilot's day begins early in the morning. Wake-up calls are usually sometime between 5:30 a.m. and 7:30 a.m. Most pilots kick off the day with a morning workout. Regular exercise is required for all members of the military. Staying in good physical shape helps keep troops healthy and gives them the strength to complete difficult tasks.

On days when they're not on flying missions, pilots often spend time training. They might log hours in a flight simulator. Flight simulators are a lot like highly detailed video games. Some of them have full **cockpits** that look and function exactly like the ones in real aircraft. Large video screens use computer graphics to show what the pilots would see if they were flying real planes. Flight simulators allow pilots to practice flying in new conditions. They also help pilots get a feel for new aircraft before actually taking off.

Military pilots must train to handle other tasks while they're flying. Most military aircraft are equipped with weapons, communications equipment, and technology for gathering **intelligence**. Modern aircraft are often equipped with guns, bombs, and missiles. Communications equipment allows pilots to stay in contact with one another in the air and with their commanding officers on the ground. Intelligence-gathering equipment helps pilots collect important information such as enemy locations and the layout of unfamiliar territory.

On some days, pilots prepare for future missions. They study intelligence to learn everything they can about the locations where they will be traveling and the enemies they will encounter. They might study enemy aircraft and weapons in order to look for possible weaknesses in their foes' equipment and battle plans.

Pilots also prepare for missions by keeping a close eye on weather forecasts. Weather conditions can have a major effect on how a pilot flies. Pilots must know if they should expect storms, extreme wind, or anything else that could affect the way their aircraft operate.

Mission days are often the most exciting parts of a military pilot's job. Some missions are routine operations that pilots will perform many times throughout their careers. Others are once-in-a-lifetime events. Flight missions can take place at any time of day. They can happen anywhere in the world. Pilots must be ready to tackle any situation their commanding officers place them in.

Before taking off, pilots must make sure that their aircraft are ready to fly. They check to be sure that all of the aircraft's equipment is working properly. They also make sure any necessary gear has been loaded onto the aircraft. These preflight checks can take up to two hours to complete.

Once a pilot takes off, it is his or her goal to meet the mission objectives. Objectives vary from mission to mission.

During mission briefings, pilots learn where they will be flying and what their objectives will be.

Some missions are based around tactics that the military has been using for many years. For example, Army pilots use transport helicopters such as the CH-47 Chinook to move ground troops to where they are needed. Air Force stealth bombers drop explosives on enemy communications equipment to make it harder for them to organize their plans. Some missions are conducted to gather intelligence. This information helps U.S. military leaders make better decisions as they plan their attacks.

Different types of aircraft are used to complete different types of missions.

LIFE & CAREER SKILLS

Modern aircraft are equipped with a wide variety of safety devices. However, this technology is useless if a pilot doesn't know how and when to use it. Military pilots spend a lot of time in safety training. Flying aircraft can be incredibly dangerous in peaceful situations. It is even riskier in combat missions. Extra safety training can be the difference between failure and success in an important mission. It can also be the difference between life and death for many pilots.

Other missions might require pilots to use tactics that have never been used before. As technology advances and political situations change, military leaders are forced to think creatively. They must find ways to deal with new situations they encounter.

A pilot's work does not end when the mission is over. After landing, pilots must inspect their aircraft. They report any problems to a crew chief. The crew chief is in charge of aircraft maintenance. The pilot then gives a mission report to his or her commanding officer. Pilots often discuss their missions to see what went right and what can be done better in the future. The commanding officer might offer feedback to help pilots improve on later missions. Once they are done with all postflight activities, pilots are sometimes given a few days off to rest before they start working on a new mission.

Before and after missions, pilots must check their aircraft for problems.

CHAPTER THREE
LEARNING TO FLY

J oining the military is a life-changing decision.
It's not something you should do simply because flying
airplanes sounds like fun. Working as a military pilot is very

*Members of the military often go for long
periods of time without seeing their families.*

dangerous, whether you are flying peaceful missions or fighting in a war. It might also require you to travel around the world at a moment's notice and spend long periods of time away from your family and friends. Anyone who is considering joining the military needs to consider whether they can deal with these aspects of military life.

If you are considering a career in the military, talk about it with your family and friends before making a final decision. You can also talk to military **recruiters**. They can answer any questions you have about serving in the military. Anyone can get advice from recruiters without making a commitment to enlist.

Once they have decided to enlist in the military, future pilots must think carefully about which branch they would like to join. Each branch offers different career opportunities. Each also has slightly different requirements for becoming a pilot.

No matter which branch they choose, all future pilots must be at least 18 years old to enlist. They must be in good physical shape. Each branch measures the height, weight, and body fat of those who want to join. They also screen for illnesses or conditions that might prevent people from doing certain jobs in the military. For example, each of the five branches requires pilots to have good vision. The exact requirements, however, vary from branch to branch.

Members of the military are organized into two general groups known as enlisted troops and officers. Enlisted troops join the military by signing up and going through training. Officially, you do not need any previous education to enlist. However, the military rarely accepts people who have not at least finished high school.

Officers help plan missions and serve in various leadership positions.

Officers are the leaders of the military. They move up in **rank** and take on more responsibilities as their careers develop. There are several paths to becoming an officer in each branch of the military. Only officers can become pilots.

Most people who plan to become officers do so while getting a college education. They can attend the U.S. Military Academy, the U.S. Naval Academy, or the U.S. Air Force Academy. These colleges combine traditional education with military training. Students earn bachelor's degrees in a wide range of subjects while also developing the skills they need to be leaders in the military. All students become officers after graduation. Admission into these colleges is extremely competitive.

Students at other colleges and universities can work toward becoming military officers by joining the Reserve Officers' Training Corps (ROTC). In addition to their regular studies, ROTC members participate in military drills and training exercises. They often receive **scholarships** in return for their service. They become officers upon graduating from college.

College graduates without previous military training can become officers by attending Officer Candidate School or Officer Training School in the branch they hope to join. These programs last up to 20 weeks and provide college graduates with the skills they will need to succeed as officers.

LIFE & CAREER SKILLS

It can be very expensive to get a college education. Joining the military is one way to help make college more affordable. Each branch of the military offers scholarships to help its members earn degrees. Some of these scholarships cover 100 percent of the cost of going to college. While you shouldn't join the military simply to get a free education, it's an important thing to consider if you are thinking of a military career.

The Army is the only branch that does not require a college degree to become an officer. High school graduates have the opportunity to become warrant officers. Warrant officers are slightly different than other types of officers. Instead of taking on new responsibilities throughout their careers, warrant officers become highly focused experts in a single field. Many high school graduates become warrant officers so they can learn to fly Army helicopters.

New members of the military who hope to become pilots must first pass physical, mental, and written exams to make sure they are qualified for the job. These tests show whether people are able to deal with stress and make

Army helicopters are the only military aircraft that do not require a college degree to pilot.

decisions quickly. They also make sure that people who want to become pilots have the knowledge and reasoning abilities they will need to make it through flight school. Military leaders also take other factors into account when selecting candidates for flight school. For example, they look for officers who had high grade point averages (GPAs) in college. They also prefer candidates who have science-related degrees.

Even experienced pilots must continue training to improve their skills.

Previous flight experience is helpful in being selected for military flight school. You can get this experience by taking flying lessons at **civilian** flight schools.

The exact structure of flight school varies slightly among the branches. However, they all have the same basic requirements. Flight school students spend many hours in flight simulators before they take off for the first time. Students take their first flights with experienced instructors. After many hours of practice, they are finally allowed to make solo flights.

In addition to flight practice, pilots spend a lot of time in the classroom. They learn about different types of aircraft and how they work. They also learn how to read flight maps and operate communications equipment. Safety lessons help them learn how to respond to any problems they might experience while flying.

Instructors carefully monitor each pilot's progress in the air and in the classroom. These observations help them decide which types of aircraft each pilot is best suited to fly. Pilots then spend time becoming experts at their chosen aircraft. Finally, after hundreds of hours of practice flights and months of classes, they graduate from flight school and begin active service in the military.

CHAPTER FOUR
THE FUTURE OF FLIGHT

There are more than 1.4 million men and women currently serving in the U.S. military. The military is always looking for new, qualified recruits. However, it is almost impossible to predict how many people they will need at any particular time. There is not always enough room for everyone who wants to

Military training also provides pilots with skills they can use in civilian jobs.

join. In these cases, people who want to join the military must put their names on a waiting list. At other times, the military needs more people than it has.

Pay in the U.S. military is based on rank and years of experience. As a result, salaries vary widely. Officers make much more than enlisted troops. For example, enlisted personnel at the lowest rank with no experience make just under $18,000 a year, as of 2011. An officer at the lowest rank with no experience makes almost $34,000. Experienced officers of the highest rank earn more than $225,000 a year. In addition to their base salary, members of the military can earn bonuses for having special skills such as knowing how to speak a foreign language or being able to operate medical equipment. They also get allowances to help them pay for food, clothing, and housing.

The military offers excellent retirement benefits. All members can retire with full benefits after 20 years of service. This means that they can retire at a young age compared to most other careers. Many people who retire from the military find new jobs in related fields. Others go back to school to earn more advanced degrees. The military often helps retired members pay for their education.

Pilots who wish to find new jobs after leaving the military have many options from which to choose. Their unique training prepares them for jobs that most people aren't qualified to perform. With a little extra training, they can learn to fly large commercial jets and become airline pilots. Others become private pilots for corporations or government agencies. They fly businesspeople and government leaders to important meetings around the world in private jets. Some former military pilots use their knowledge to help companies develop new aircraft technology.

It is impossible to know exactly what the future will bring for military aircraft pilots. Because of changes in politics and technology, conflicts could happen almost anywhere in the world. **Engineers** are constantly working to develop new, improved aircraft. The military will need skilled, hardworking pilots to fly them. Are you up to the challenge?

21ST CENTURY CONTENT

The military sometimes offers bonuses for people who have special skills needed for current operations. For example, the United States has recently been involved in conflicts in Middle Eastern nations. Most Americans do not speak the languages of these countries. As a result, the Army began offering a $35,000 bonus to speakers of these languages who enlisted. By keeping up with current political events, you can learn which types of skills the military is looking for and take advantage of the bonuses they offer.

Will you become a pilot one day?

GLOSSARY

aircraft (AIR-kraft) vehicles that can fly

civilian (suh-VIL-yuhn) not a part of the armed forces

cockpits (KAHK-pits) control areas in the front of aircraft where pilots sit

dirigibles (DIR-i-juh-buhlz) aircraft (blimps) that are shaped like cigars, filled with gas that makes them rise, and powered by motors

dogfights (DOG-fites) battles between fighter planes

drones (DROHNZ) unmanned aerial vehicles that are operated by remote control

engineers (en-juh-NEERZ) people who design and build machines or large structures

intelligence (in-TEL-uh-juhnts) information gathered and used by government agencies to plan and make important decisions

maneuvers (muh-NOO-vurz) difficult movements that require planning and skill

rank (RANGK) official job level or position

recruiters (ri-KROO-turz) military personnel in charge of signing up new members and providing information to people who are interested in joining the military

scholarships (SKOL-ur-ships) grants or prizes that pay for students to go to college or follow a course of study

stealth (STELTH) the use of silence and secrecy

FOR MORE INFORMATION

BOOKS

Anderson, Jameson. *Fighter Pilot*. Chicago: Raintree, 2007.

Loveless, Antony. *Fighter Pilots*. New York: Crabtree, 2010.

Williams, Brian. *Pilots in Peril*. Chicago: Heinemann Library, 2012.

WEB SITES

America's Navy—Careers & Jobs: Naval Aviators
www.navy.com/careers/aviation/naval-aviators.html
Read about the process for becoming a Navy pilot and find out what to expect once you've finished flight school.

Marines—Marine Officer: Fixed-Wing Pilot
officer.marines.com/marine/winning_battles/leadership_positions/air/fixed_wing
Watch videos showing the different aircraft used by the U.S. Marine Corps.

U.S. Air Force—Careers: Pilot
www.airforce.com/careers/detail/pilot
Learn more about what it takes to become a pilot in the Air Force.

U.S. Army—About the Army: Warrant Officers
www.goarmy.com/about/service-options/enlisted-soldiers-and-officers/warrant-officers.html
Find out more about the process of becoming a warrant officer in the Army.

INDEX

ABOUT THE AUTHOR

Josh Gregory writes and edits books for kids. He lives in Chicago, Illinois.